BORN TO LEAD

H.E Mohammad Abdullah Al Gaz Al Falasi

The World Leading Influencers

Dr.Hala El Miniawi

Table of Content

Acknowledgement 1
Introduction 4
Chapter One: My Story 6
Imaginart Narration By Mohammad Al Gaz 6
   In The Beginning 7
   The Companions 16
   Dried Lemon and Spices 23
   The Arabian Gulf Titanic 30
   The Flow of Fortune 39
   Politics and Economy 48
   Saying Farewell 55
Chapter 2: Never to Be Forgotten 62
Narrated by O. H Al Gaz 62
   Thorough Our Eyes 63
   Those Were The Days 71
   The Future Can't Wait 78

Chapter 3: My Memories with Al Qaz Family 82

Narrated by Amna Gareeb 85

    The Blessing of His Company 86

Chapter 4: A Model In Business and Parenting 94

Narrated by Khalid and Khalfan Al Gaz........................ 94

    A Journey OSuccess…………………………………100

    Intellectuality anenlightenment……………………...108

BORN TO LEAD

ACKNOWLEDGEMENT

I forward my book to all those true leaders who inspired me to write about their endeavor to make a difference in a world full of paradox. The hero of this book, H.E Mohammad Abdullah Al Gaz, realized his purpose so early in life and persuaded a big dream till it became an actuality.

The simplicity of the life he lived, the profound impact he left on his surroundings, really surprised me and at moments brought tears to my eyes.

DR. HALA EL MINIAWI

Yet the joy I felt while reliving moments of his experiences were so enriching that I feel so excited to share it with my readers.

This book comes as a result of my deep realization that what humanity needs during those difficult times is a memoir of what truly makes a leader someone to remember. We do need to recall the originality of our creation and the purpose of our existence.

For the hero of this book, it was evident he wanted to leave a deep imprint wherever he could reach. His purpose was fulfilled and it continues to be a legacy for those who followed him and a torch of enlightenment for others who strive to be the ones who build the world, connect hearts and minds, and wait not for rewards.

BORN TO LEAD

DR. HALA EL MINIAWI

INTRODUCTION

This book introduces the real influencers whose deeds are changing the world by means of their goodness and real endeavor to change the life of their communities to the better, creating an everlasting impact on people and society.

The aim is to give the new generations role models of true leaders who devoted their life to share the blessings they have with others.

BORN TO LEAD

Those who build the world though humble enough not to show off their greatness. Those whose giving knows no boundaries, away from the spotlight, waiting for no rewards. Those whose deeds extend the borders of egoism, moving from individuality into togetherness...

Those whose deeds bridge hearts and minds.

Who are they?

DR. HALA EL MINIAWI

CHAPTER ONE

MY STORY

IMAGINARY NARRATION
BY
MOHAMMAD AL GAZ

BORN TO LEAD

IN THE BEGINNING

In every successful business journey, there is the finishing line that once you cross you become a winner. When raising your hand as a champion it becomes a compulsion to recall the starting line and the roads you crossed with all of their hardship just to light the torch for others to reach their destinations. Each one of us has his own moments of triumph and failure, those moments that would shape our characters and pave our life paths. Those ticks are usually linked to images of people who helped in determining who we are. Places usually form the setting for most of our life occurrences as they might influence our destiny though we leave our imprints on them consecutively.

The Arabian Gulf formed the background for most of my beginnings .As a child, the roaring of the waves advancing then retreating leaving behind its white foam on the powdery sands of the shores were quite scary to my innocent sensitive heart.

I used to run away in freight till the warm strong hands of my father taught me not to fear loudness.

That tall fisherman spent most of his days in water and found in the ocean his only way of earning the few coins that kept us alive.

He used to drag me back to the coasts that constituted part of my destiny. His hands were coarse, full of scares with his veins popping up through his dark skin up to his arms giving him the strength he needed to pull the fishing nets.

Those were mostly made out of bristly ropes interwoven in a way to gather what the generosity of the sea could afford to our humble family.

In his tender attitude he would lean down to gather the sea shells scattered half buried in the sand encouraging me to do the same.

 Feeling my little soft hand in his, gave me the courage to form a deep friendship with the sea that continued to be my companion for a long period of my life.

At those old days I was a good observer of what the people were doing, how they gathered their ropes and how they pushed their boats down the tide while singing a repeated rhythm that kept their minds awaken.

DR. HALA EL MINIAWI

Their power of endurance was greater than the hardship they were witnessing on every sunrise they left their places to face the unknown.

When I grew up and it was time for me to adopt the craft of my father, my trail of harpooning and fishing was not a great success .It seemed that fishing wasn't meant to be my real pathway.

 The sea was high at that sunny day as I was moving up and down with the little wooden boat, leaning at its edge trying to get good hold of the fishing net with its fortune of sparkling silver fish, hurtling against each other in a desperate attempt to escape.

My immature hands couldn't really hold longer and out of a sudden I was overthrown into the water. A panicked fish slashed my face with its sharp tail. The pain in my left eye was unbearable as I tried to make my way back to the shore .

BORN TO LEAD

That happening marked a new phase in my life as my fate had a different twist from that of my Dad.

Fishing, then wasn't meant to be my way of earning a living and I had to look for other venues though there were very few possibilities. Life was very hard at that time in the Emirate of Dubai in the Thirties. People either worked in diving for pearls or fishing and both options were not suitable for me. I had to think of new ways though for my young mind the sea was the only destination.

The separation of my parents that followed was inevitable as it seemed and I had to move to live with my Mother at a different Areesh with my grandmother.

We developed a unique relation that was a mix of disciplines and ambitions molded in a pot of the unconditional love that Allah has endowed upon me as Mohammed Abdullah Al Gaz in the form of the marvelous woman Salama my mother.

She was the support and the relief from the hardships I witnessed throughout my passage till I landed at the safe shores of prosperity.

To her I was the only son and treasure that she fought with all her power to inspire and push to the top while to me she was and continued to be till the last day of her life the blessings and the real cause of all the success I achieved.

Her presence in my life was the source of inspiration, and the light that enlightened my heart, mind and soul with the values that constituted my personality, shaped my behavior and attitudes and made me the man whose net was full of fortune yet he was always ready to share it with others.

For any individual, whether poor as I had started, or wealthy as I ended, knowing the purpose of our existence and the real values that we should stick to, constitute the core themes of life itself.

In Al Ras, an old area of Dubai with few scattered houses on the creek I lived my teenage .I attended Al Mutawa and learnt the Holy Quran. The Mosque nearby, though very humble at that time was the most tranquil place that gave my soul its resort.

Bowing and kneeling in adoration and worship of Allah our creator, was an act of feeling the extreme harmony with the universe , placing my forehead on the tender soil of earth , releasing all the negative energy and regaining the balance I needed to continue.

Faith was the key that opened all the locked doors for me as I could understand the cycle of the infinite law of giving, whatever you give to the world would come back to you. It is definitely our acts that determine our success in a series of causes and effects that go beyond our simple understanding.

Our intentions and deeds are monitored and seen by Our Creator as we are disclosed. Then the more we help others the further we relief ourselves and support our purpose.

BORN TO LEAD

Life in the Thirties in Dubai was very simple with rarity of resources, aridity of land and harsh life conditions.

DR. HALA EL MINIAWI

THE COMPANIONS

Y̶ou need to keep the company of good friends whom you can trust .You would support each other in business and life .You remember Moses in The Holy Book when he asked The Mighty God to support him with his brother in his journey .You don't have any brothers or sisters, your friends can be the ones"

My mother Salama whispered in my ear as we were strolling along the shores that stretched from

BORN TO LEAD

Sharjah to Dubai as there were no roads or buildings, just the azure blue sea with few palm trees and dispersed Areesh huts here and there.

The serenity of that scene continued to dwell in my mind from time to time as it was associated with the warmth of a Mom's compassion that coated the bitter facts in a wrap of tenderness which made the impossible eligible for negotiations.

Hard times can lead you at a certain situation to a locked path that neither your wet nor intelligence could guide you through. In such a case changing the place could be a solution and that was how we left Dubai to Al Bahrain, a neighboring country with better chances for trade provided at its modest markets.

The great woman who happened to be my mother devoted her time for making Al Burquo, a type of cover for the face that women wore at that time and she used to sell them to her neighbors and friends.

At that time I worked in different jobs and collected a small amount of money to start my own trade.

We headed back to Dubai with few Rupees earned by lots of hours of hard work in difficult weather conditions that veered from extremely hot days at noons to dry windy nights that whistled through the cracked door and windows of the old house that hosted our stay.

At some evenings I would venture to go out for a wander on the beach. The waves roaring was no more terrifying as before but it rather gave my mind a rhythm as it used to tide and ebb giving me a chance to immerse my footprints on the sand then sweeping them away in an instant leaving nothing behind but the white bubbles and a memory of those thrilling moments that would never be repeated.

During my stay in Al Bahrain I learnt my first lesson in business as I was multi - tasked, working in different jobs to gain experience and collect the small budget I needed to start my own trade.

Dealing with a diversity of traders at the port and in the narrow old allies of its bazaars I knew how important it was for a merchant not only to accept all the different cultures but to understand their preferences of goods and merchandise as they constituted my customers and give me indications of the trends in the markets.

My second message of business came from Salama my mother when she advised me to have a group of trustworthy friends who could be my partners. Following her guidance I had a great inclination to surround myself with friends, I gave them the sincerity they deserved and they never failed me.

My cousins were the men whom I could trust with my family during my traveling. They were another blessing from God as they accompanied the whole of my journey in life and continued to be the brothers I didn't have biologically as I was the only son of my family. They were modest, calm, smart and very good listeners.

They were able to gain the confidence of people so easily due to their transparency and straightforward manners.

Then my friends were my support and I have chosen a trustworthy faithful one as the right choice to become my partner in my trade journey to India and Pakistan.

BORN TO LEAD

*Al Mutawa was the teacher in the old days in Dubai in the Thirties.
He taught the offspring reading, writing and the Holy Quran.*

DR. HALA EL MINIAWI

Dubai Creek was the venue through most of the trade deals were done. It constituted the vein of life for the whole of Port Saeed, ALRas and the other areas.

BORN TO LEAD

DRIED LEMON AND SPICES

Trading with India in the sixties in Dubai was the best known way of starting a business .With the hundreds of Rupees I gathered from my work in Al Bahrain I started my first trip to Pakistan trading dried lemon for spices. The Dhow that was a large wooden boat with two storeys was our means of transportation. There were different types of those dhows but we mostly used the Boum or the Bhugla that sailed vigoursily through the Arabian Sea heading to the coasts of the small towns and cities scattered on the Indian coast.

The journey itself was a hard trip and an adventure at the same time .It needed the endurance to bear long hours of staring at the water below splashing away in fluffy clusters or gazing at the infinite horizon where you could hardly identify the sky from the azure sea in clear daylight . Such patience I witnessed very early in age while watching my father and his friends of fishermen and pearl divers and I could figure out then that persistence was a major factor of success .It seemed my mind was sub-consciously trained to accept hardships, physical and mental, as a price that any efficacious trader should pay to ensure a better life for his children and decedents.

Reaching those small coastal towns on the way, was a real relief as we used to plunge into the humble souks, trading our dried lemon for spices .Those were the moments of negotiations when we used to hammer down the prices to get a deal .

I still remember the white teeth of the Indian traders shining through their smiles with the salty drops of sweating dripping from their faces, once we raised our hands to shake theirs in agreement. That was exactly what I enjoyed in trading, dealing with people with all what it carried of mixed emotions, wets and even humor at some situations. Then developing those feelings of belonging to a community and living those interrelated webs of relations that connected humans.

I could always recognize the wisdom of creation in creating different demands and offers, that once realized would definitely complete the whole image of trade exchange. We were created different to complete each other like pieces of a puzzle, that fit together to form the whole picture of a meaningful living.

I felt belonging to the sailors who pulled the ropes and raised the mist. I sensed it with our comrades on the boat as well as with all the others I met.

One of my friends once said to me:

"God had bestowed on you this marvelous ability of compassion that you could identify yourself even with a hungry child we met in the souk, let alone the poor traders whom you helped from your own pocket though you didn't have much to spare .But to be honest I had always admired you when you do that as it carried a promise that Heavens would reward you back" My friend phrased it well as he was able to understand me all the way.

BORN TO LEAD

Yet what he described as showing empathy for others was really meant to feel the joy of sharing with others the blessings I had even if it was a piece of bread soaked in oil and dried fish powder that mostly fed us on our long sea voyages.

Dried mango pickles that would sting your tongue with its sharp taste releasing all the flavors in one burst, was the treat we got after we finished a deal and got our boxes stuffed with goods.

Never had I felt any type of self-pity when I recalled moments of hardship as I had always viewed problems as triggers meant to create in my mind new alternatives .Such solutions would open new doors that might have never occurred to me before.

"There is wisdom and goodness in whatever befalls a person with faith. The God of Heavens and Earth will never fail a true believer's expectations" Salama my mother used to tell me and I knew that better days for sure were to come.

DR. HALA EL MINIAWI

Traders and merchants were displaying their products along the shores, near the creek and in the traditional souks and bazars that made Dubai a hub for trade since the early days even before the discovery of oil.

BORN TO LEAD

Trading with the neighboring countries was done basically through the sea that connected Dubai with the world. Simple wooden boats and the human factors were the main sources of economy at those days of the Thirties and Forties.

DR. HALA EL MINIAWI

THE ARABIAN GULF TITANIC

We were in the Sixties when life in Dubai was most vibrant along the sides of the Creek. Human activities filled the shores of the azure shallow waters with goods while dhows of different sizes floated on the coast or sailed on their ways to the Indian Ocean. The murmuring sounds of traders bargaining would change into grumbling but not for long as those crowds as diverse as they were had in depth the same purpose, they wanted to earn their living. At those days I moved from the Areesh to a simple home of clay and mud in Farij Bu Naser in Al Ras as I got married and was blessed to have children.

My feelings of lonesomeness as being an only child was replaced by the great joy and gratitude for God for the blessings I experienced .My daughters were a joy to watch with their plaids swaying around while they were playing with the cloth dolls they had .My sons were the pillars I needed to build a small empire of mine whose doors will remain open for all friends, relatives and even strangers who needed help or support.

With a large lovely tribe at home I continued my trading trips to India with my friend. The sea dizziness and the blurring hot sun became part of my daily routines.

My community of friends and neighbors got larger and I was known for my readiness to help other people.

They would knock at my door early mornings or late at night and I never complained as I knew that the more I gave to the world the more I got in return.

It wasn't always the financial benefits that I sought but rather that fulfilment and satisfaction that filled my soul with serenity .The worst battle had always been the one you fight with yourself as your inner voice would encourage or blame you and that mostly what determines your destiny.

I lived with the people of Farij Bu Nasir as I breathed the warmth of the tender misty muddy walls of my house .We used to sit under the palm trees in one Areesh which was built as simple

Majlis for the males while the women were making bread, Harees or Majboos.

We literally shared our sorrows, worries and the simple joys .I knew the names of their children and told their teenagers my tales of the sea travels.

Such social bonds were nearly unbreakable as it was a means of survival for our society in a period of history when resources were very limited as the aridity of the bare lands, the shallow shores and the humid tropical weather gave no hope of cultivation.

One day in April 1961, MV Dara which was a British vessel landed at Dubai creek shores. Hundreds of people got on board the huge magnificent ship to explore its elegance not knowing the tragedy that it was hiding. Some other families from Farij Bu Nasser embarked at the broad deck with their children aiming to travel to

Karachi while Bu Hani accompanied me on a trading trip to Bombay.

It was such a gloomy day as the sky was grey with dark clouds and the wind was blowing sturdily. The sea waves were roaring against the shallow shore which forced the captain to drift the gigantic liner and sail into the sea to avoid the instability of the shorelines .Out of a sudden a rumbling explosion shattered the middle of the ship apart .A big hole was opened in the top deck from which fire blazed out creating a massive panic in the mob of people who were gathered on board, as they started throwing themselves into the slashing waves.

 Many lifeboats were thrown into the water but the overflow of the frightened crowd fighting for their lives made survival impossible. In a desperate way to aid many mothers who lost their children in the crowd I found myself overthrown into the roaring sea. I surfaced to see the fiercely blazing Dara drifting rapidly away and spent the next two hours fighting to keep my head above water.

It was rough and the waves were breaking over my head, so I was treading water with the waves behind me. Before dawn I spotted what at first seemed to be a shark but turned out to be an oar with a corpse draped over it. The body slipped off and the oar kept me afloat for a while before I fainted away.

When I opened my eyes again I found myself in a hospital in Al Bahrain. Soon I regained the heartbreaking scenes I witnessed on the disastrous MV Dara. I recalled the panicked faces of men thrashed into the sea , the screams of mothers frantically calling for their children and the lost kids searching for a strong hand to cling to during such terrifying moments.

DR. HALA EL MINIAWI

For the first time in my life tears of deep agony started to drip from the corner of my eyes slipping into my beard leaving its salty sour taste on my lips. In another moment of awareness I remembered my companion and my heart was comforted by his survival.

Meeting my family again was a joy though deep in my heart the anguish continued knowing that around 289 people died in the Dara drowning and among them many families and friends were identified.

The saddest story was that of a woman in the neighborhood who came to ask about her young sons who were travelling to Karachi and were never found. I could never tell her the truth about their death.

Such a crisis as miserable as it might have been ,yet it gave me a new feeling of deep commitment to my hometown and the people to the extent that once my feet touched the shores of Dubai my heart pulse were so vigorous yearning to meet my family while my tongue was murmuring in whispers prayers of gratitude to Allah for my survival .

DR. HALA EL MINIAWI

The MV Al Dara drowning in 1961 was considered a big tragedy as hundreds of lives were lost. Mothers were separated from their children and many traders never came back to their homes. Mohammad Abdullah Al Gaz was on the ship and was miraculously saved to find himself in Al Bahrain

BORN TO LEAD

THE FLOW OF FORTUNE

My trade expanded and my trustful relations took me into a partnership with Juma Al Majid. We worked together in textiles trade then moved to a new type of merchandise of electronics.

During that period I moved to Port Saeed, a vital area near the creek. My house had a separate Majlis (Guest Hall) and my door had always been open to all types of merchants and businessmen who came to Dubai as it started to boom after the primary findings of oil .It was then that I moved to a new domain of trade .I studied the flow of electronics into the markets and the great demands on buying appliances .After careful planning and negotiations with my friend and partner Juma we bought franchise of several international brands including General Electrics ,Samsung, Philips and others.

During that prosperous period I came into acquaintance with His Highness Sheikh Rashid bin Saeed Al Maktoum. I accompanied him in most of his travels and became a kind of diplomatic advisor. At that time I moved to Al Himriya area but kept my devotion and good relations with the old neighborhoods that witnessed my modest beginning.

When I heard of a restructuring plan of the whole Hamadan area, my main concern was to provide residence to all those families who were to be evacuated.

The generosity and deep love of the people that Sheikh Rashid showed for all those around him had granted me an area in HorALAnz in which I designed and built houses to host more than 75 families. Consequently I started working in property, land planning and construction .That was partially due to the great devotion I had to my city Dubai .Such deep belonging and loyalty grew to enclave the whole of the UAE after its formation in 1971.

Sheikh Rashid was a unique leader, visionary and highly dedicated to serving the nation. His visions extended the present to the future and in cooperating with Sheikh Zayed Al Nahyan, they were both able to create a big dream that turned to be an actuality in a short span of time.

I had been a witness and part of such leap of faith that changed the country from merely a landscape of sand dunes, shallow watered shores and few palm trees here and there into a business Haven.

They had true brotherly relations, they agreed on laws that would boost trade and attract foreign investments and they invested a lot in building a solid infra-structure that would support the progress they aimed at.

I never allowed myself to have any feeling of superiority even when I was in the company of great rulers .The more God bestowed on me of money, children and grandchildren, the more I felt humbled by His graciousness.

I continued to build mosques wherever I settled. Going at the early dawns to pray al Fajir prayers with my sons and neighbors was a ritual that never seized to form a basic part of daily routine that lasted till the last day of my life.

The basic forth rule of business and life success that I had always reminded myself of was never to be allured by the illusion of being better than others by means of having the power of money or authority.

I deeply believed that those blessings were granted to me as part of my mission in life to serve others. Reading was my own way of keeping myself on the track of self-growth as my mother Salama had always advised me to. I read all types of books and assimilated their content that through time my intellect was gaining a wealth of concepts, philosophies from the ideas that survived for thousands of years on pages of plain paper.

DR. HALA EL MINIAWI

In every line I relived the experiences of all those who travelled, parted, got lost, returned or never found .The faces of people asking for help in the places I visited on my trading travels, never parted my mind so I ordered the doors of my big house to be kept open providing support for all those who needed help.

The sea with its high waves, tides and ebbs, resembled human nature. It would rage and calm, proceed and retreat, swipe and sway like a giant. Yet for me it was a good companion as I understood its mood. At times, the sea waters would swift smoothly with the light breeze, transparent like a crystal that reflected the colors of the rainbow .At others it would take me high and splash me on shores I had never dreamt of .Yet I learnt how to surf its wildest waves and survived because I knew that in every mile I sailed I had

Mother Salama praying for me and my children were waiting for my return.

Deep in my heart, my inner voice never stopped praying for Allah to keep me safe for my family and community .I knew my purpose so neither the sea roaring nor its calm whisper could divert me from my determination to succeed .

I greatly contributed my attainment of all what I achieved to the satisfaction I always had at all the blessings that I shared with those around me.

DR. HALA EL MINIAWI

Port Saeed played a great role in improving trade along with the free taxes trade laws that Sheikh Rashid Al Maktoum adapted in the Sixties to boost economy in Dubai

BORN TO LEAD

Sheikh Zayed Al Nahyan and Sheikh Rashid Al Maktoum had a future vision for the UAE and their dream became a reality

DR. HALA EL MINIAWI

POLITICS AND ECONOMY

Politics are the roles we play to help people live in better conditions." I used to explain to my sons as I had always tried to raise awareness in their little minds of the importance of the community welfare in simple words they could understand:

"I learnt many facts from the books I read and acquired many others from the experiences I passed through as I travelled to many places and met many people .I witnessed their pain and sufferings and I promised myself throughout my life to provide help for other human fellows. You know my sons what makes you wealthy? It is not the golden coins but how you spend them to help others live a better life"

I used to point from my window at the construction works being held everywhere in Dubai and say:

"That's how our leaders are building the future for you and the other youth"

Sheikh Zayed said:

"The livelihood is from God, the money is God's, the land is God's, the grace is God's, we are all God's creation, and he who has trusted God will never be failed, and those who come to us are welcome"

Those moments I used to spend with my children were the blessings of God that I had always acknowledged in gratitude.

I would recall their childish acts and laugh at the amount of innocence they had in their little hearts.

Once my Mother Salama returned from Al Umrah and my little son was very excited at her return and wanted to give her a gift .In his innocent attitude he brought his coins and gave them to her .Funnily enough he came back next day and asked to get his money back as he needed them to buy sweets from Bu Bakeer.

We used to remember that story and laugh in happiness at his real desire to share what he had and show affection to those who were very dear to his heart.

My young daughter used to welcome me with her lovely imaginary stories and juvenile talks and then she grew to be one of the pioneers in providing charitable services to others.

My son Khalfan was my mother's Salama favorite son as she called him after her father .As a token of love she used to give him extra pocket money of which he used to share it with his brothers and sisters .That was the early sign of his inborn traits of resilience and assertiveness. He grew up to be my assistant in my business and proved to be a great figure in the field of business and charitable services.

I used to remember my children acts and behaviors and thought of these as indicators of future attitudes. I had tried to plant in their little hearts and minds the core values of the deep belief in Allah through reciting The Holy Quran and learning Al Hadith and transcode such religious teachings into daily practice of tolerance ,compassion and endurance.

The ethics of being truthful, forthright and helpful to others were the basis that I tried to raise my children on. Learning and education as well as the value of work were among the best practices that I highlighted throughout my life as through my readings , encouraging my daughters and sons to continue their higher studies , and contributing to building schools during the early stages of teaching in Dubai.

As they grew up I could see how children were really affected by the endeavors of their parents.

"We mirror the world to them in their childhood and then they project that on their lives later on" Being human and supportive to other people, were the morals and ideals that I have treasured the whole way of raising my children and it had succeeded in creating a legacy of the respectful, honored and the dignified way of living they adopted in their life..

BORN TO LEAD

Mohammad Abdullah Al Gaz had been a close friend and a wise companion of Sheikh Rashed Al Maktoum. They worked together for the welfare of the UAE

DR. HALA EL MINIAWI

Sheikh Zayed Al Nahyan and Sheikh Rashed Al Maktoum joined hands to build a prosperous country for the nation. Their Union is still celebrated providing the world with a role model of real brotherhood

SAYING FAREWELL

I continued to play many political and economic roles in serving my country and the people. All the decisions I took even those related to adopting the Dollar instead of the Rupee as a reference currency during my work as a vice president of the central Bank in Abu Dhabi , were based on a deep analysis of the market and the future trends of economy .

The death of my mother Salama was a big blow to my heart. We were never separated the whole of our life unless for short periods during my business trips. She was the first person to meet whenever I enter my house. Her face had been my mirror and her wisdom and unconditional love were the reasons behind all of my success. I wanted to achieve milestones to please her and wherever I went she was backing me up at home .When she was gone I felt a big space in my soul I tried to fill with prayers knowing that death was meant to bring us closer to the real core of life.

Death is an upgrade of life to a better level where there is no pain, neither agony but rather releasing the soul from the restrains of the body to fly in the realms of Heavens' Mercy by God's well.

Our precious human existence is too valuable to be wasted once our bodies decay. Our soul transparent as light, vibrant as the pulse of our hearts, difficult to analyze or touch, will undoubtedly persist to exist in a better horizon where beauty is complete, love is eternal and the reward for our deeds on Earth is redeemed..

"When you think of how valuable your life is and the limitless options it carries, you will find all the means to achieve the possible, and what might seem impossible.

Keep in mind the immortality of your soul and the continuity of your existence in a place where pain, agony, envy and all the other feelings that hurt, will no more prevail." I said to Khalfan my son who was weeping his grandmother in silence as he was her favorite grandson.

Many years passed since my separation of Mother Salama, so many things happened, new marriages, new births and novel experiences of happiness, tiredness and joy molded in a pot of deep appreciation of all the things I could accomplish .

DR. HALA EL MINIAWI

I feel I have reached the end and fulfilled my purpose on Earth.

My body has become feeble though my mind and soul are still vivid with my consistent prayers for the Al Mighty Allah that in spite of the pain in my lungs my tongue still repeats "Glory to Allah, Praise and blessing of His Name.."

As I was on my way to the Hospital in Abu Dhabi, I glanced at the scenes below and said farewell to the places that witnessed my childhood, teens and old age. The land features had changed dramatically yet the Azure blue sea has kept its glow.

I passed by Al Wahida where I left my sons and daughters with their families in the care of Allah, The most Merciful. Then I could spot HorALAnz, Port Saeed, and The Clock Tower .The areas where most of the buildings carried my prints.

BORN TO LEAD

Beit Al Kheir, the charity association I initiated with my sincere friend Juma Al Majid would continue along with my other charitable endowment to spread my message of commonality and social care.

With the last breath I took, my sons were around me and my daughters were hiding their tears. Memories started to drop, it was time to leave .I knew that this was the path Mother Salama, my wives and my two daughters had gone through."

"To Allah we belong and to Him we return"

DR. HALA EL MINIAWI

Mohammad Abdullah Al Qaz had left a legacy of charitable endowment .He left the world with a content smile as he believed he had fulfilled his purpose in life.

BORN TO LEAD

DR. HALA EL MINIAWI

CHAPTER 2

NEVER TO BE FORGOTTEN

NARRATED BY THE DAUGHTER OF MOHAMMAD AL GAZ

BORN TO LEAD

THOROUGH OUR EYES

"My father had a tender personality but at the same time he was decisive, resilient and Charismatic"

O.H the daughter of Mohammad Al Qaz said while staring at her Dad's photo and recalling the best of her days, those she spent as a child.

"I remember the big Majlis that used to host my Dad's friends .Only my adult brothers were allowed to join them while our Mom stayed in the kitchen to help in preparing the sweets but after they went to the mosque to perform the prayers I used to get into that big Hall. It was amazing, spacious and with lots of interesting things for a child .I loved drinking from my Dad's glass and even tasting the leftover from his plate .He was someone so dear to my heart. Someone whom I won't disobey even in the tiniest decision as buying sweets from Bu Bakeer who used to come every week bringing Halawa or frozen yogurt on his cycle.

Every morning we used to say greet Grandma Salama and she used to give us our pocket money before we went to school.

As a teenager my father was a role model for me .He had a daily routine that started early at dawn to go to the mosque with my brothers and our neighbors.

Then he used to have his breakfast and at eight sharp he would go to his office .By mid-day Dad used to come back home, have lunch, pray then he would resort to his room to read. My father had a large library of all types of books which were all donated to the Cultural Center upon his request. After AlAser prayer Dad used to go to the farm in Al Khawanij

"Father had never treated us differently from our brothers the boys .He used to love us his daughters and shower us with gifts when coming back from his travels. The big bags of textiles he brought from India, Pakistan or Europe were displayed for the females in the family to choose what we liked .Then Mama Salama would distribute the rest to relatives and friends.

DR. HALA EL MINIAWI

The big gate of our big house in Al Himriya were always kept open for visitors. During Ramadan, the kitchen was kept open before sunset with food like Harees served to whomever liked it for Iftar.

Grandma Salama was a unique woman, powerful yet full of sympathy for the less fortunate women who attended her gatherings. She was a resourceful woman, wise and unprejudiced that women in our alley trusted her and listened to her advice.

We were not allowed to attend the talks of the elders though there were times when we all listened attentively to her stories about her family history. Her faith and reliance on God were so great that it was reflected in all of her manners and behaviors. Her praying beads were sparkling in her hand while sitting on her praying matt waiting for Al Azan to pray.

"Our home in Al Wahida covered a large spacious land with three main 3 gates. The North gateway opened to the shore with a balcony and wide windows to allow in the soft breeze of the sea .Most of our rooms were on that side. The South entrance opened to the neighborhood and it led to the main Hall, and dining room that was open to all the old ladies who used to spend hours with Grandma Salama and even spent the night in the guest rooms. Omi Sheikh used to stay for months with us teaching us Al Hadith of The Prophet Blessings be upon him and we went to Al Mutawa to learn reciting The Holy Quran..

The Third Doorway was devoted to a separate building Al Majlis where my father hosted his guests .In the backyard there were certain stables for our cows who were milked by certain workers so we got fresh milk every day.

DR. HALA EL MINIAWI

Yogurt, butter and cheese were made at home and we the girls in the family were allowed to watch the process .

BORN TO LEAD

The closeness of houses in the old alleys invites you to a tour of discovery of the intimacy and warmth of people who could share their own space with others who were in need.

DR. HALA EL MINIAWI

High minarets, the old stones and bricks and the flying pigeons in open yards tell stories of the spirituality, human bonding and peacefulness that kept those places alive in our memories.

BORN TO LEAD

THOSE WERE THE DAYS

"Spirit of the past never dies as it dwells in our mind like magic .Never shut it down as it is part of who you are"

The flow of memories is really what keeps us connected to our roots .I recall the image of Grandma Salama preparing the milk pudding with Saffron that my Dad loved .The Ferny, as it was called traditionally, was the treat that all the family children used to await in the large yard of the kitchen .We used to lick our bowls to the last drop pampering our taste pods with its deliciousness. GlabJamo was another type of sweets that our Indian Cook used to prepare as its big balls of dough immersed in syrup would resolve in our mouths leaving us carving for more.

Those little moments of joy that used to make our hearts throb for more of family bonding were really meant to cherish the spirit of togetherness then as we grew up we carried out those chores .I used to prepare Balah Al Sham sweets for my Dad's guests while Umi Amna baked Al Jbab Bread ,Al Harees and Al Thareed.

Respect, self-control and cooperation became part of our daily life routine that included lots of rules to govern our eating habits, sleeping and going to our farm in Al Khawanij area where all the fun activities were hidden for our little limbs to be indulged in.

BORN TO LEAD

The farm had rows of palm trees that were very dear to my father. The three floorboards building that hosted our family , the old ladies from the neighbors ,and the children of Bu Yousef and Bu Hani my Dad's best friends ,was a huge construction with a ladder that connected its storeys .A big swimming pond promised us all the excitement and the adventures as well. Crickets and lizards were accepted as part of the deal as the whole surrounding was basically sand dunes apart from what had been planted of lemon trees , mango and the palms my Dad's favorites.

Such spacious spaces gave our childhood the freedom of running, swimming and staring at the clear sky at night decorated with the twinkling stars glittering like pieces of diamonds spread on a velvet cloth like the dress a bride might wear for her wedding.

DR. HALA EL MINIAWI

We would get up in the early dawn by the smell of Al khamir bread prepared by Umi Amna on a grilling tin placed over a fire in the yard .Mom would have made Al Chami cheese served with dates and the dough mixed with saffron and cardamom to make khabees .Our gatherings with Dad was so precious that we would sit around him listening in adoration to his virile voice telling us stories about India, Egypt, Oman and Al Bahrain. He was our window to a world that we were yet to experience within the span of our norms and traditions.

Grandma Salama replaced him in his absence and she was the resourceful woman to solve all our issues. Once we were playing with sand when a huge venomous snake popped up through the cliff behind my sister.

BORN TO LEAD

We were all frozen in our places out of fear then Omi Sheikha came running and calmed us saying that we shouldn't move. We stayed still for a while then the snake retreated in defeat to its hidden pit.

DR. HALA EL MINIAWI

Cooking over an oven of bricks, food was prepared in huge amounts to serve guests and friends especially in the month of Ramadan

BORN TO LEAD

In the Forties and Fifties, women covered their faces with Al Burquo and wore the black Abbeys. Yet they played important roles in raising their children and forming the social bonds that kept their culture and norms revived

DR. HALA EL MINIAWI

THE FUTURE CAN'T WAIT

My wish to join the University was so great that I interrupted my Dad's reading time one afternoon. He looked at me hastily as he was really absorbed in his book. I told him my wish to continue my higher studies and for my great surprise he agreed.

Years of study passed, I graduated, worked in teaching and then got married and had children.

Dad never ceased to be on my side listening, encouraging and supporting.

Al Khawanij farm expanded to host Mohammad Al Qaz children and grandchildren .The only son of Mama Salama was blessed to have an extended family that compensated his lonely childhood.

My Dad became a father, a leader, a social reformer and a man who gained the love and adoration of all those around him .His humor kept us entertained though his smile disappeared for days at the death of Grandma Salama ,he regained his lovely temper though at that time a sad look was hidden in his dark brown eyes.

He kept her memory alive by the charity endowment entitled to her name and the prayers that never seized to be his habit till his last days.

My Dad gave me a collection of the best of his palm trees and told me to keep his memory vivid

DR. HALA EL MINIAWI

by praying for him and I knew he meant it to be a reminder of the great value of charity. I deeply believe that unveiling the depth of his humanitarian attitudes would be the best tribute I can pay for his memory.

The schools he built and the charity Beit Al Kheir continue to inspire us to follow his footsteps. The real legacy he left us was in the positive attitudes he inspired us through his insistence to trust people , himself and the belief that all what befalls a believer is meant to make him a better person and that our destiny is never bound with its beginning but by its ending.

BORN TO LEAD

What makes a true leader is his ability to envision a future even if its outlines were not seen in the horizon

DR. HALA EL MINIAWI

The past could only change by the toil and hardships that the ancestors took as their duty for the future to be ours

BORN TO LEAD

Dubai today still keeps the same land features of the Creek, the dhows and the shores but after transformation

DR. HALA EL MINIAWI

CHAPTER 3

MY MEMORIES WITH AL GAZ FAMILY

NARRATED BY AMNA GAREEB

DR. HALA EL MINIAWI

THE BLESSING OF HIS COMPANY

She received us saying "Welcome, Ya Hala WaMarhab" Umi Amna as Al Qaz family called her during the 20 years she served as their Nanny. Then she started reciting lines of poetry that read like this:

"Give me the pen to write my poetry... Don't waste the Time..

BORN TO LEAD

I will send a letter of salute... To the one who deserves the Thanks..

To him the master of our home... Whose open-handedness is known to All..

May God bestow on him.. Abundance of wealth. Sons and Heirs..

For You Mohammad Al Qaz I rhymed my words and expressed from my heart ..All the Gratitude..."

The old respected lady allowed her daughter Fatma to serve us the same food that Al Qaz liked in his life time .Their hospitality really was humbling yet the feeling of love that prevailed was so overwhelming. She started telling me about her journey of 20 years with Al Qaz family.

"I wasn't working for them, I became one member of the family. I remember the first time I started doing my job milking the cows which seemed rather an easy duty. I approached the first plumb one standing in pride in her stable and was trying to reach out to its breast when suddenly she kicked me away that I found myself stuck to the wall and that remained a joke to laugh at for long.

Mohammad Al Qaz and Mama Salama were really concerned about my safety and such compassion was showed to all people, animals and even plants that happened to be lucky to be in the circle of Al Qaz attention.. Later I learnt that Al Qaz cows were pampered and looked after by and I was trained how to do the milking in the proper way.

Cooking was my other task and Mama Salama with her praying beads in her hand guided me on how to prepare food with affection. Moving around like a princess, I would calmly taste this, stir that, add little salt or saffron yet always doing things quietly and elegantly .I learnt that food would get its positive energy from those who prepare it.

The children of the family were my responsibility as well. I used to escort them to their schools and when they wanted to buy sweets from Bu Bakeer. Al Qaz sons and daughters were so polite and disciplined.

Respect was the dominant role that governed all our relations .Certain daily routines were considered as rituals.

No one was to be excused from the family gatherings for lunch and dinner during which Al Qaz used to tell jokes teasing the little ones then patting on their heads while listening to their stories with great love and tenderness.

He was a very kind master, humble and modest though very punctual and concise in his demands and orders.

DR. HALA EL MINIAWI

Al Qaz generosity was outstanding especially when I used to be the first to tell him of the birth of a new healthy boy or girl. His eyes would be lit with joy as that special smile of happiness enlightened his face."

"Our trips to Al Khawanij were full of adventures" The old lady continued with a lovely beam on her face then she continued:

"In the early mornings I used to bake AL Riqaq bread on the grilling tin. Its delicious smell would awaken the children as they would gather around me asking for some even before breakfast was served.

Then our excursion in the spacious farm with the children would start. Running here and there they might trigger a hornet nest .The wasps would fly everywhere after the fleeing kids .Someone would have a swollen eye or ear from the bites.

BORN TO LEAD

At night I would escort the girls to the roof as they would lay down and count the stars, tell jokes and laugh till our hearts ached.

During Ramadan, the fasting month all the blessings happened .The family big house at Port Saed was just like a beehive as the demand on food starts from sunset to sunrise.

Al Qaz females along with my daughter Fatima would plunge into the making of Fotor and Sohor for almost my master's guests, the workers and other passersby. The Minaret Azan would be our alarming clock announcing the start of a new day of fasting.

Life has changed a lot since those old days. You can see the great shift as you look at the Creek and afar at the high buildings whenever I recall my memories with Al Qaz family, I feel the happiness that we lived."

DR. HALA EL MINIAWI

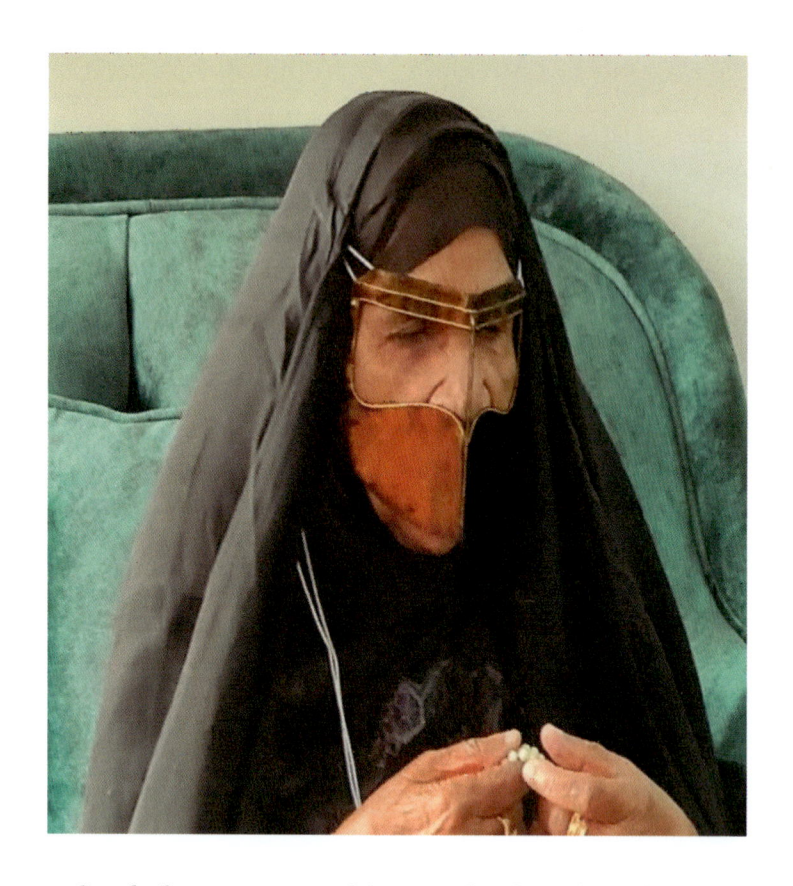

Souls have no wrinkles as the loyalty of the old lady embodied the core values of life in the past in the UAE and how those ethics still connect people to their roots and heritage.

BORN TO LEAD

DR. HALA EL MINIAWI

CHAPTER 4

A MODEL IN BUSINESS AND PARENTING

NARRATED BY KHALID AND KHALFAN AL GAZ

A JOURNEY OF SUCCESS

"Dad was a story of success that should never be forgotten. Since my childhood he was supportive and inspirational in a distinctive way."

Khalid Al Gaz started recalling his sweetest memories with his father.

DR. HALA EL MINIAWI

" I remember him saluting me when coming back from the kindergarten .I used to come into the house hesitantly as I didn't like to show my young age .He used to be with his cousins in Al Majlis .Dad would just say in his manly voice :

"Look at Khalid coming back from school, he is in grade One .What a smart son I have!"

"His words meant a lot to me as I felt he was sensitive enough to understand my feelings and helped me build myself esteem through his continuous encouragement .His high expectations of my abilities and what I could achieve were the real reasons of my success at work in my career later. Dad was also keen on nurturing a sense of responsibility and how to fulfill our duties .Once he asked me to deliver a package to his office , I handed it over to his driver since he was going there My father called me and explained in his composed attitude that one's man errand is never another man's duty .

In Al Khawanij we used to spend the best of time in his company. With his praying beads in his hand, he would stroll along the rows of palm trees holding our little hands, helping us to climb the tree trunks to pick some dates and feel that sense of achievement that he was very keen on implementing in us by all means.

Faith had been a success factor in my father's journey as it gave him the tranquility he needed to deal with people from the different trends of life. He was a companion of leaders and travelled on diplomatic trips with Sheikh Rashid Bin Maktoum

God bless his soul, yet he never lost the humbleness and modesty of his character that made him loved and respected by all those around him .He would greet his workers and ask them about their families and would help solve the problem of anyone who might approach him for help.

Was he idealistic then? In a way his noble values were kept untouched as he had a very high code of ethics that he applied to his family, work and relations. At the same time he followed the logic of things and was able to study the fluctuations of the markets demands and act accordingly. His intuition was very high that he had really that true instinct that would tell him what to do at the right time.

I was really amazed at the way my Father treated his employees. He was so generous and compassionate. He would always remind us that those people left their hometowns to come and work hard to earn a living so we were supposed to help them feel at home and support them in all possible ways. Mohammad Al Gaz, was a compassionate father who contributed to the development and emotional growth of my character .He left us a legacy of benevolent endowment and many charitable services to provide to the world to keep the continuity of his mission in supporting all those who needed help before they ask for it .As such his memory will remain to dwell in our hearts, our deeds and in the minds of our descendants"

DR. HALA EL MINIAWI

True Charismatic visionary leaders encourage transformation and adopt change

*Our good deeds is but a continuity of the mission
that our ancestors have started and paved the
way for us to continue*

DR. HALA EL MINIAWI

INTELLECTUALITY AND ENLIGHTENMENT

MY Father was a humanitarian leader in the way he viewed life and people ."

Khalfan Al Gaz started talking about his father with a great deal of love and adoration.

BORN TO LEAD

A great reader as he was his knowledge of literature, history and politics was outstanding .His travelling, trading trips and meeting people, expanded his horizons of thought and intellect that he wasn't confined with the restraints of the present but rather learnt from his experiences to put plans for the future .His strong relationships with his friends and companions were based on his ability to accept the others.

A concept derived from his great faith and assimilation of his religious teachings as testified in the translation of Al Aya 62 Sorat Al Baqara from the Holy Quran :

"Those who believe (in the Quran) and those who are Jews ,and Christians and the Sabians and whoever believes in Allah and the Last Day and does right , shall be rewarded by Their Lord , they have nothing to fear nor shall they grieve ."

I learnt from him the importance of helping other fellow humans acquire education to become better individuals in their societies . With the help of God 2 schools were built in Dubai during the Eighties when schooling was at its earliest stages .

The mission of providing humanitarian services was never confined to a place, so other schools were established in other parts of the world.

Another important aspect of my father's character was his reliance on the power of logic .He deeply believed in the power of the Human mind to understand the Universe and find solutions for the problems and sufferings of the people whether that of poverty , shortage of fresh water or health care.

Parents are those who teach us about the world and help us experience it in the right way. My father's journey was that of hard endeavor that resulted in great success by the favor of Allah.

BORN TO LEAD

His political, economic and intellectual roles were rewarded by the good reputation he had, the love of all those around him and in the legacy we vowed to carry out of supporting the welfare of humanity worldwide"

DR. HALA EL MINIAWI

The great well of people to change their life conditions to the better with their hard work can make a huge difference

BORN TO LEAD

The journey of progress and prosperity of The UAE was started by great leaders who had a future vision and worked hard to achieve it. They remain the inspiration for many generations to come.

DR. HALA EL MINIAWI

Testimonial

The author would express her greatest appreciation and gratitude for O.M Al Gaz who accompanied the journey of writing this book. Without her detailed tales of the past, the book would not have carried such authenticity. The gratitude is forwarded as well to Khalid and Khalfan Al Gaz who shared their perspectives of the unique character of our hero

Mohammad Abdullah Al Gaz Al Falasi

1930-2016

Printed in Great Britain
by Amazon